Unpleasable Nature

Unpleasable Nature ©2020 *by* **Crista Siglin**. Published in the United States by Vegetarian Alcoholic Press. Not one part of this work may be reproduced without expressed written consent from the author. For more information, please contact vegalpress@gmail.com

Cover art by Crista Siglin

playtime with other

7 The Red of Anne
8 When We Are Outside, in the House
11 Playtime, As

falling in a falling shape

25 Nine Alterations
27 Carving
28 Shrine
29 Undue Division
30 It's Got To Be New
31 My Shoes Grow Dusty (not with soil)
33 Advisory in an Irish Movie Theater
34 Soon
35 Round Goings
36 Short Chapters
39 When the People Had Seen Enough
40 Request(s)
41 Confound It
42 Gaping at the Midnight River
43 Closure
44 Broke Weather Break
45 New Dis Ease
46 Recording Holes
47 Strange the Flame
48 The Fever of a House
50 Once She Busted
51 Open, Hiding
52 Alter
53 Get the Boy One Anyway
54 I'm Laughing into the Corners of My Unpleasable Nature
55 Anonymity
56 Every Moment
57 Finnigan's Rainbow

58 Divorced of Divorce

59 What Was

60 More than Once

61 A Pause

62 Catch

63 Meeting

64 A Moment Along, Alone

65 No, Not This

66 4:46

67 *Yesterday*

68 Expectation, Or

69 Rehearsal

70 House Paint

72 Eavesdropped, Paraphrased (a thing between two pianos)

73 Remembering For

74 All Untouched

75 Untitled

76 The Burning House Has Few Rules

77 Different Ways of Saying the Same Thing

78 Falsity

79 Repetition

80 Prayer

81 How Long a Road You Have in Those Feet?

82 Impossibility Grows into Night

83 Jacob's Ladder

84 Pink

85 Sauna

86 The Kitchen Floor Was Fitting Once

87 Quiet

88 Uncover My Covering

89 Another Round

90 Where is My Imagery

91 Goodbyes

playtime with other

The Red of Anne

Anne, ravenous & red / took it / during her continuous vacation away from her needless want for a place to be seen inside of, made a pulse / young man's cock / she watched volcanically as palms danced over his head as a hurricane premonition / it was the only dream / she had had for an entire year/ once she made enormous / a tire swing / swinging into distant days gone from her / having told mom / she played doctor with the neighbor kid / after tap lessons / even around velvet / leotard sequins loud & red / in the hot afternoon / once the sun hit red / back shed / behind the house, she put a stop to that / right quick / & Anne became / red & no longer little pink cheeks flashed quick with / glances to catch / if she was to be caught / never told her mother / anything / after that, later / Anne would make her valentines large sealed / hearts shaped by paper cuts on her / forefingers / she gathered them all about her but would not give them away / to her interests / instead draped her / hair over them / before she slept / red on red / on through dreams marooning / her to the middle / a bed too large for her alone / she would get older every night / & sometimes leave / in the night / get into her car / find the water tower / red & spotlighted so the / dark couldn't touch it / but she would / lean against it with / all the pressure / on her chin / it'd be a little apple / she'd think as if she were her own / orchard / not part of a family / or larger orchard / never / a part of the cider / she'd feel strange / such thoughts were not red / like her / & she'd wonder who / she needed to love / in order to get out / small town dump / all the things that were not red / thought about having a baby / thought about wanting to have / a baby / but thought shit / I can't stand the blue / set off with a different / thought south / even while knowing / nothing really special comes / taking a thought south / but she figured /might find / body of water / throw herself in / she did read once / people couldn't always see / blue, & so they'd describe / the ocean as blood, wine or both / & she could already feel the pressure of watery garnets on her hips / she imagined it / Anne's always been / the beholder of red / finds an empty / suitcase / every place / she goes to find more red / 17 suitcases full / so far / to the brim with red / & all her stockings / not quite rouge / when comparing her knees to one another and to / the knit she rolls up / with red string / one suitcase / she found all flowers / that were not / red but could be made / to be / the trophy / of this particular collection was baby's breath that shone vermillion as she poured / the bottle of Coca Cola / she found in Alabama / James Dean had touched / all over / another suitcase got filled / with maraschino cherries while / Anne sang / Glitter and Doom / through rural Louisiana / till she could find / a bar that she would not leave / fortnight of red / walls & reckoning / glances from staff / shirley temples traced / dark red bourbon at the bottom / she had another suitcase / for every tequila sunrise she'd shared / with someone wearing lipstick / anyone wearing lipstick / she'd talk seriously about taking them / with her / push forward into a / frontier of red sand / & cactus blossoms / but instead / she would leave before they'd wake & before / the light would start / onto the horizon / taking napkins they'd dabbed carefully / at their lips / stash them away with / promise of / we'll see each other again / one day, / it could have been / she was delirious / but she was only / cold and no / red was to be found / in her hotel room / so she turned on / the television / saw how the west was one / big bowl of dust / put on her last pair of shoes / laced up the last red she wanted to take care of & / left the door to the room / wide open with every suitcase / ajar & bits of past / red blew up / stuck to the paisley / walls & hours / after / she left / fluttered out after her as if they hadn't noticed / till then because / she did leave quickly / as she always leaves quickly, but they too were surprised / like everyone else / on account of not having realized / that life they'd been given / from the endless / & terrific / red of Anne

When We Are Outside, in the House

I

Francesca & I are pulling each other's hair

    we are in the bathroom

    we've never cleaned

she says my hairs belong to her pelvis

I say hers belong to my armpits

    by the afternoon

    we are bald & crying

we are grown men now

we are old men now

    I tell her she has nice tits

    she grabs my ass

we have nothing left to lose

    we play catch

    with a broken polaroid camera

my toss hits her in the nose

    she bleeds

    she sweeps the floor

    with wisps of her beard

II

Francesca and I begin
singing songs
about when we found
your imagination
in a seal's coat
you had buried
by the peonies
in the backyard.

She sings
how she wanted to drop it
next to the sleeping figure
of her love
so that he would wake,
and they would peel
oranges until dusk.

I sing
That you nearly drowned me
as I tried to smell you
underwater because
I thought you dear to me.
I sing
that you were never
born into the fables I sing.

We sing
that we will not be returning
your skin to you
until you have nothing more
seven years
and we have
no more
reasons to be
digging.

III

Francesca and I are playing mommy/daddy

        in the dining room

        in order to stop the rumor

        of sweetness in the soul

I say

        I am not a woman scorned!
        I am a wilderness of syllables!

She says

        I am something that's got to be awakened!

Then the thought of a naked man enters the room.

        He carries a glass fisherman's weight.

        He shoves the small sphere into the small of Francesca's back.

We scream.
We run to the doll house.

        We try to hide inside
        the small of the attic
        but it is full

of stiffening tissues.

Playtimes, As

I

Unica & I go dancing
                              come back all sweaty
              Unica stalls   in the stairwell
                                      I stare at her stalling
              She pleads
                      says nothing

                              I tell her it is time to go to bed
                      She says *not now*

I ask her why
        she says it's got to do with the lavender in the bathroom
I tell her she is stupid
   tell her lavender is the biggest crime of nature

        She's upset & I tell her I was kidding
                        about the stupid part
She tells me to tie one long string around
        every one
                of her finger tips
I do it because I still feel bad

she says it's not tight enough, won't leave her tingling
        the tips gotta get COLD cold

                                ghostlike like an orchid
              I tell her it's well-cold-enough
                              we're not yet in the flat
Unica sneers   *I ought to have known you'd be so frail*

        in retaliation, I wrap her   with my arms
                    past the point
I can wrap anyone;   lose feeling
   keep holding, keeping hold   she capitulates
              I drop us both
              angry & pooling & so
              she calls out for men to pull us up

              they laugh from the other side of the wall, so
              we die like orchids do
                                        falling soundless shrill

II

Eva and I go   to the barn
          start kicking the shit out of
every kickable thing we see

hay bales, kicked
garden tools leaning, kicked also
                  down now, ha

gloves on the side of the railing
          kicked & flying out the wide   wide door
                  ha ha ha

Imagine their hands
          she's gasping
Ha ha ha ha
                  Imagine HANDS were in there

Ha ha ha
          Whose hands, though, Eva?
His hands!
Ha ha ha
Ha
laughter fades   kicked out too
          as it does when there is
                  no thing
                  left more to kick

III

I chatter as the dishes chatter but Emily is silent
                while she washes them, but
           fills gaps in chatter with quiet moaning

First time washing dishes?
              It's a silly question & she treats it like one
        moans louder
moans till the kitchen gets too small

                    that good-sized blue glass I like cracks in the water
                            when Emily busies herself with the silverware
not having been disrupted, a little blue glass of blue glass mends into suds
                quietly, cleanly
                      cutting no one, although
                            we know it could

IV

Octavia & I pull weeds from the garden
        dandelions, mostly, Octavia
                wraps the stems in aluminum
                        dips the blooms in bleach
                                & we watch their splintery petals disintegrate

she lets them behave as though they are alive
        positions them perky in nearby wheelbarrow
we say prayers to outer-space
we holler when space doesn't answer
        she makes up a god & says I can't use it if my person is not ready

        I say okay and wipe the dirt off my hands

V

Claude is at the frame shop considering
              only frames they can fit themselves into and
     through

            they will only buy as many frames as they have selves

problem is I cannot count variable selves while they
move through such variable frames

& Claudes' pockets are not so deep as to be able to contend with
            purchases of ever-variable sizes

                they scold themselves

into one or two selves
      that can be
           more rigidly framed

VI

Paula says she will KILL ME kill me
         & I believe her

                she made a model of the event of killing me
I am before a drawing I made of her painting & it is all wrong and I am positioned
         in gruesome light
                     looking all deciduous & green &
                  smokey
                          as a premonition

                donkeys & demons & rats & animate semen
                     run oblong
                     round me

       she apparitions me (more than a little
                             violently)
             & now, I can say,

            I am happy

VII

Maya has a habit — stretching
   eternally
      as we walk

                                      down
               a sidewalk
               outside
               her apartment
        it gets old because
it slows us down
          & more
time, you know,
     makes one old
          but now look here see
we're fearsome delight
      & streaking strides of glamour
          mirrors and women made
          nearly naked, shining
               monument words of nothing

& now
forgetting
& now
      overheard panic dropping

VIII

Cindy takes polaroids of me taking polaroids
                      in her bedroom
            I do the same, her way

wow
        really really cute
                  what we've done
                here
                        let's cut 'em up real small

we do
we do

                we're married now, but don't know who got married
all adjacent women in the room start to talk
                  so we make disguises
                    lazily
                        they see us still
                            under the hats
all kinds of hat, all kinds
                        of head
                            we're shaking
                                we're tickled

                            with everyone we've come to know

pretend you never met me
        & you only see me just now

Cindy is not naked, but I am & am
                getting ready to make a suggestion
                            she notices (my breath, getting ready)
                                licks two photo bits, sticks them tenderly
                                    onto my tits

IX

Dora writes three books of self-referencial philosophy
        places them in the window sill

& sleeps
I watch her, get bored, wake her up
        licking the vertical expanse of her back

                      when she is good & awake
I tell her her books are compelling objects
            sitting in the afternoon
                  sunlight like that
            delighted, she demands
        we watch two or three movies with plot points
of **trickster get even**

        he's dumbly painting in the next room
(she would tell you who *he* is)

        we replace his little things with other little things

to get him
        get him back

                real good

X

Leonor wraps every inch of me in scarves
pastel, all of them
                    Beckons me to look a look
to appear
        to manifest
Somehow
I can't   she hates a quitter
I can't
                    she installs a camera in my room
                            reckons I'm lying about how much I can't
                                    appear

XI

Toni rips the doll right open

       I wouldn't call it horror
but the look on my face makes her pause a moment

              silently she pulls out a couple more stitches
                      hands me two eyes of an uncertain size

this doll is and isn't you, and you can sit in the middle with it

I swallow the eyes
feel them descend my body non-dramatically

Toni says she's sick of me and I can't blame her

              takes the whole of the room in her arms
                        & I go down

                    elsewhere

XII

Doris claims
time is a moving
object
        a moving
                object is an idea
ideas go limp
                limp without containers
expression
        is container
I tell her I am myself at times
        an expression
                communication
        sending
sending is
difficult
                it's difficult with no body
nobody is a body is
a body   is not a sufficient container
                & so I lost
                time to growing
                up to be anew
        apart from her stoic chairs - stacked & silently falling
she looks away, I look at her looking away
anew, away, again

falling in a falling shape

Nine Alterations

I

with, around, about, inside / technology, you are outside it / it is inside / foreign
it is not / absence calling / you to stone / to the eyes of flowers / impeccable
cheekbones of riverbeds / vestige of a lesson / scores of images
interrupted condemnations / consider / when you eat
rotten strawberries / a bowl of fresh milk
does not follow

II

sphere of soap water / melodic paroxysm / bent air, bent / waking dream / a garden
confuses, leaves you / alone / your stick and looped rope / limp, swaying
ennui / a mouse grows long teeth / plays / dead, teeth exposed
the mouse remains / still / death waits for the mouse
who plays dead / an aroused string
distracts the cat

III

your hair does not become you, you become / your hair is damp / cold and smelling
shampoo / a memory / misbegotten complicity / plays with the ends of it
you become the end / the ends play with you / broken glass
underfoot / small vertabrae sounding–as one
might imagine / constrained grief / sharp
dampened / a hungry animal waits
its nose / deepening your palm

IV

idle revelator / grief is here / just sits / no veil intended to be lifted
a girl speaks to sheep / drinks herself frozen / there was no one
just sheep / no love where she treads / no one
translates grace / she is terror / disgusted
she dances there

V

nosferatus turn tears to diamonds / we're swimming /our bodies thin
sharp / the TV tower / God / speaks / in the 3rd person
so as not to startle anyone / I worry
for unsent postcards / to keep
the sky from falling

VI

a chair's design is important for the mood / it strikes when it is empty / one could be tempted
to say waiting rather than empty / a chair waits for no one / it sits
on its own / considers its mood

VII
no returning home / I've been known / loss of breath / beneath sheets
a strange bed / we part / my mouth shut / no air escapes / nothing
so blameless as a glass of water / no need to apologize
a glass of water says sorry before the door / ajar
water sees you / in everything
everything / in itself

VIII
infected moon / glowing, pained / trees gathered / round its pate / becoming
a hole / that old woman / kneels before it / I watch / behind
an illness / pouring into her

IX
the sky made itself / obscene / diner of the 50's, trampled confetti / the Sistene Chapel
half its image missing / only Adam hovering / broken pair / scissors / a split
becoming a knife / smiles kept for the dog / smiles
scared of meaning something

Carving

isn't it so free or isn't it
so small with the rest of us

sad death
concealing concealment

morning conceals flowers
tremors of openness

speeches cut short by tears
become real inside their walls

snarling obsession, staying
words, keeping words

so long so long
carvings fade

so long the tree, alone
memory of the thought

thought fades, but not
entirely its obsession

Shrine

san maximon / on the wall, or in the
closet, amid smoke / smoke / smoke
of a glaring kind / while i am
fucked in the ass / with
gladness

no afternoon light / it is night, now / for sweet dreams
scarcely shame / in the moon, she made darkness
tolerable - what a pity / tonight
i appear unholy

i believe this mind / badly / believe me
i steal actual thunder / handfuls
electrons screaming

Undue Division

breath ballooning my belly
I wonder how I feel tomorrow

attention divided, not
altogether unpleasant

I recall sweated smell, &
now swells focus

associating you to a TV show
I never watched & this

moment is slight
a torment in two parts

It's Got To Be New

this metaphor
falling is falling in a falling shape
this is
not new
we've broken the rule
the rule is to name a pattern we like, is to break
those who break the rule
to stand in the corner if we, ourselves do
if I am not already in the corner I will not
stand there
did you arrive here willingly?
do you stay here?

My Shoes Grow
Dusty (not with soil)
   after George Oppen

my shoes grow
dusty, not with soil
      & one does wonder how
one becomes one
      distant -
how alone alone
can be
      the bridges slow
            themselves into eternities
      rain into endless rain

          unarranged, we become

          intermittent
blooms of buildings
building into sky
      rubble

            producing concavities

          forget musculature
          or never know it
we don't begin ourselves
soil does
this growing
dirt of soil
      soil of water

& dirt &
      not moving so much
& not so much today
or yesterday
who can say what
of tomorrow
          or of the next sequence of
what is this moon
& space between
      hunger & sleep
that part of the bed we unconsciously
fought for
      made wild accusations
of morning for
in the morning
who recalls the colors of their dreams
I can cry of relief
in the airport yet still

crave you to look back
                    I miss my father again
I miss you & I never thought
I could see you like this
         I wish it could have been more,
                more honest, honestly
this all
      repeats itself
in my days I feel
quite abandoned but by whom
who was there to begin with, other
than I?

my feet grow disproportionate to the sky
again the sky & feet
the verticality disappointing
        & recollection of now so unimagined
but I imagine it becoming more
layered than the next now
who wants the next now
        now now, I want now
but it has come to pass
so exquisitely
that I should never
                have it.

Advisory in an Irish Movie Theater

fear of a moment
passing will pass
a moment spent
in fear & pass
the fear to the next

passable moment
it is today tomorrow
I am back but the
musicians are still
in circle, discussing

beware the shock
of cold water
remain calm
this will lessen your
risk of drowning

Soon

soon, enough
soon, I come
slowly, though
but in good time

soon, all there
the old woman
stayed to the rain

something says
there was never
a sun, on this day
there is no day

Round Goings

you enter
a scent bright
in the shape
of the thought that never
fully comes—but you do
recognize it as a sensational
body of its own
you've concerned
yourself with finding
every impossible method
for peeling an orange/you die
it reveals itself to you

Short Chapters

I

I raced the sound
my own feet falling
a fit of flowers
tantrum's footrace
no opponent
we fight
for an audience

II

I am held up, not
breathing
I enter a house—party of gold people—
I, too, gold as I leave a falling night
my entrance is lit, the hallway
breathes with me—first time in hours
or days—
I fall to the floor

III

I do an apology
waltz
in the apology
garden
wearing apology
pants
apologetically
swaying
to the song of
sorry
but I'm so sorry
I cannot
go on sorry
for long

IV

I want to be inside
my rage, but invite myself
ten thousand miles
out, even I feel the invitation
dampened
dawn is here with me—I've
intoxicated
myself, and my self is now
violent, or just
irrationally affectionate
sweet, hot
bitter
almost puts me back
into the world but
I lie down on the ground
rest with the sun
remembering its face
to the horizon
the shape of everything
answering the shape of a new
day and it rolls over
pressing me down

V

once I had a very lovely
a very nice time

the color of tree
excretions
Vermont in the fall
although I have never been
there, I knew what it was
that—thick, slow and
going down—feeling
in confidence

knowing nothing except that
once I was a sap—my love
a thing—everywhere close
to everything, even
my short fingers

so much touching
even the finest items inside
your mother's home

and you, now
outside her body

yet never reaching
out of her mind, and so
I moved in

VI

dry—cracked again
an examination of my toenails
I find gross standing
with myself
I am a synonym for anything
dirt and scant seeds
tender headed dandelions
tired by bully August
incessant, slow
how strange to see ugly
in a gentle light
how strange to see my feet
loved by you, how strange

seeing you are mine
now, I stand tall and lovely
above now
my nameless toes

When the People
Had Seen Enough

it scarred as before
breaking skin
this realization
I would have had them
walking on all manner of
soft
for-
eh-
ver-
last-
ing
from the earth
below
low this
earth to what
it gains nothing from its position
it has been
some
thing
untethered
but for imagining
these
little
names

Request(s)

perform to me how
I perform to you

a childhood
friend's face

a long lashed
boy on the u bahn

how long ago
tragedy shapes

a different kind
of story, kind of funny

I have been unkind
like "her kind" - like

gravity absent from
the surface of water

Confound It

confounded, I tell
time by a
confound of swans
as they sleep

chaotic on the canal
and yes, a group
of swans must be
called a confound

confound it
a sink broken
is undone
retie the water

confound a glow
figuring
where the moon
ought to be

confound me, I met
a murdered girl
murdered long
before she died, and

confound that window
which should remain open
to allow the scent of
tension easing

Gaping at the Midnight River

As we wait, we sleep—
dream dreams of dreams—
we discover tellurian trinkets
anchored to the inside
of each other's mouths.
Yours opens with my lips and I find
with searching tongue
a mound of walnuts
carved into the shape of my hope.
You open mine—
with thumb and forefinger—
find a riverbed
grey/soft/uncertain
clutching dear the slight skeletons—
memories
no longer absolute.
You find still
waters in the corners
of my mouth
you dip your fingertips in/bring them out
above me and
let the water fall on my cheeks.
We wake.
You stand there—
in the fearfully dim hallway—
alert/in it all with
your skin/inevitability/the light
above your head
such brilliance about you—
years pass
my eyes adjust
to your face.

Closure

years lost gathering
things by the door

I imagine fighting
you, crossing the bridge

Epicurean delights -
rotted leaves and dreaming

of grandfather. I bought flowers
but I am not at home

Broke Weather Break

moonbroch
                monkey's wedding
virga

snow eater
                                            deciduous
                                gosssamer
        swullocking   gloriole

derecho

                    sastruga
                                                    petrichor
crepuscular ray

                          bombogenesis

New Dis Ease

a heart sounds
through the pillow
along
memories
supposed to be me

imploring
immutable questions, she
carries a disease
with childish arms

a child
she doesn't recognize a fruit
need
only be refrigerated

uneaten the day
you bring
it home

days grow long
inside a cloud - could be heat or
darkness descending or
a heartbeat caught in feathers

Recording Holes

door
        sounding shut
                      lonely trumpet
        tv tower looming
sky pouring
                blue round
looming(s)   over
        a man holds
a record   spraying

splayed smoothly, played
                                                    a record is kept
                                to know something
                (great love)

requires
                                a heart move faster
                      than the mind

                (in the mind)
                    to know myself
                    in circles ('round) a hole
in the wall - a flower
                          on the wall near the
                                      hole (is another)
                                      hole in spirit, with
                              a flower in hand
                                  the hole of the spirit

Strange the Flame

    & flower eyes
held against
the sky / undone
by the day—
        the largeness of the star
making fables
        our doings—
                when I look out
        to a field of flowers
receiving the glare
without question
        they sway, staring at me—
                one thousand
                large eyes
enlisted by silent
hyper-sex
        but do not care
for their own sexiness—
        but they notice when
                I pull back my hair,
                the broadness
                of my chest smiles
& becomes one
of their brighter strains
        a pistil inside
        suggestive
        garments,
I am strange to them
        & care for the feeling;
although small, I am
        a flame into flame—
my heart
pressed tender
        into the back
        of my breasts

The Fever of a House

we breathe in the river's upward sighs
in order to feel what it means to be a thing
that weeps through the senseless ages—
we do this when we can,
as we have no natural histories
we are allowed
to call our own
the landmarks
we know of ourselves
are largely unstudied
by everyone except ourselves
and each other
when we can manage
the courage to plea for the right
to be seen large and impervious to the
discoloration of memories
and photographs

to say we have come
from anywhere is
to speak through the crooked
walls of a dream
that we awoke from
before finding out what happened
to us and our mothers and fathers,
and to the sweethearts
of a childhood that never existed

the houses we got
to be little inside
never belonged to us
or to anyone—they had no reason
to belong to us
or to anyone. and so
now, at times, we decide
to behave as though
we have no reason
to belong to another
because our hearts
feel so rapidly changeable—
as the climates of attics
through the unforgiving seasons do,
as people move their things in and out
of those corners and eventually
through the door for good

when we want to leave
the house we do not know

how to finish
building, we put on our coats and
then seem darling and turgid
to one another and
to the paleness of the sky
and the cold ground
the naked birches' branches twist
when they feel us coming
to hide among them.
these trees cannot count
their own years—
so as they live staunchly
in the absence of forever,
they pray for those who live
in a time of fear

Once She Busted

        articulate, baseless

out a basin to climb

            carefully

                  to the rim

Open, Hiding

an infant thought/startled goldfish

passing again through

its construction

you hold your hand/second sight

to mine & mine

waits

hidden in an open field/supplicating

bed/your body inside

your body

this thought never passed/you never

reach/ full sight of the body

behind my hand

Alter

it is not that I am an alter / it is my alter / must find me
when I wake / if I am to become
an alter

begging for pardon /call it a red light
relevance / if life is not meant
to struggle / why do seeds
push through

lucky ones never lie / or lay / eyes on the room / in which
they were born / they walk in the world
as if / there are no rooms / touch
dirt and / know something
symphonic

Get the Boy One Anyway

we used to have good days
I could have been so long

so long, the

broken window looking
through the broken window
at a broken window

corner of a yes
unbridled somehow
scare me so I know

I'm Laughing into the Corners
         of My Unpleasable Nature

indentions of brick
but no real brick, the
men leaning
not delicately over the counter
I have busted the minutes
you doubted I doubted
through & now
I've got this pizza

the word on everyone's lips is

O

I've been told moths can die of loneliness
but see that gravity never worked them
my feet have never been so still

can you smell the difference of this rain?
we've sought ways to be less possessed
to run or walk is always a matter to be
discussed, but not over dinner, never
over dinner

(I knew this all along)

Anonymity

to say anything of the ocean
is to say nothing at all
specific
to your ocean, but to the ocean
of everyone's ocean & I can
hardly say I now, though I am
I am
in the milk of the milk

of some spill I cried
not to mention mothers
not to mention anything
any plant or animal

or child not

aware of anger at present
but soon will make weapons of

hand mixers/towels/jump ropes
weeds/words/glances
glancing objects

you can call weapons
toys & toys
go scattered

do not pick them up
only to scatter again, leave
my irreparable scatterings of
toys & milk & oceans
for me alone as I will not speak
of little terrors unremembered

Every Moment

sinks
it
sinks
sinking sink
I am a sink

space between
cat and window
posture, gesture

bus stop & I

ever fluctuating

I am indelible
as this sigh
of *why and how*

Finnigan's Rainbow

I am not Finnigan
I am Finnigan's daughter

he cracked his head
bending back to call
his rainbow to him

the rainbow was his head
the rainbow is cracked too

I call my broken father now
his broken rainbow too
neither can hear me

all the while I cannot recall
the name he and his
then unbroken rainbow

once gave to me

Divorced of Divorce

I see mother and father
arm wrestling
trying to settle the matter
of *who gave her those arms*

neither want my arms
to be of them

I am standing near
saying things that might stop
them mid push

the spaces between my words
are louder with intention

go, keep going
I need to know who will win
the disagreement that is
not giving me arms

I keep my arms to my sides
they droop closer to my feet with
every word I do not say

What Was
> is
>> not what is
>> yet,   how
>>> that layer
> sits upon
> now   seems

so here

More than Once

more than once
I made romantic

my romantic self no one
watching but who I made

whosoever disenchants
this body, my

mind leaves
open that door

A Pause

man   inhales
birds   f/   branches
                  protects   a hole
f/ being more   whole

while a leaf   lept
      to a
  mirror of itself

Catch

catch the ball
I made my body

bright red
a ball

beneath
head of the shower

hot water from that shower
head, I head down

catching, a spaced
out ringing

Meeting

lost before river
when river met river
river between river
a rivulet unnerved

I crack my head with
my hand and rivulet
gets excited at how
mysteriously I did it

& feels no longer
conspicuous in its
nerves, it'd all been
pretend anyhow

A Moment Along, Alone

I kill off a dozen little deer
poems & masturbate then kill

off one dozen little moon
poems, then eat pasta

unremarkably, take
off my clothes & peer down

at this, my little pasta-filled body
& consider the room & its killable

space too–everything is killable, as
in, able to be unseen

Not This

no, the cat's tail
not an incident left

unnoticed, his heartbeat
behind my ear, I realize he does not

belong to me and the realization
flushes over everybody

my body
what it is to be born

incorrectly
bound to this vehicle

4:46

& indigo lightens
branches no longer silhouettes against
a sky doing nothing but backdropping

& you are no longer excused
by yourself to be by yourself

& awake, you are treasonous
to the way you ought to be

believe the window
an actual window
& not a punched-out rectangle

it's no set, as imagined
imaginary life as imagined

real lives dreaming through the other sides
of those windows, like it or not

if you describe how you imagine them, it
could be cute, but I will tear it down

Yesterday

*It was this incident we bit
into, & it was not rotten*

just disappointingly thin

she cored an apple with
the wrong knife & got
herself real bad on the thumb

immediately got the thumb
to her lips and sucked till
it was wormish and she felt

nothing at all except
this tinge
of what was meant to come

yesterday

Expectation, Or

some suggestion of
if I knew the names
of more birds they'd stop
dying so much

some rumor of
if she'd only know her
worth she'd stop fucking
unnameable fucks

indeterminably
something which is not
said at all gains momentum &
crashes out this game

Rehearsal

off the right side
directly translated

for stage or
a language new

to me, what
me is this?

bafflement of reference
& memory ablaze

in what you said
but only

that which
I remember you saying

after you walked off
that side

House Paint

I've been what I cannot be now
        whirring
                insulated
                        insolent

only a matter of what, now
        how, now?
the mammal goes sleeping
into the folds of laundry I've
        not done

done, this calling
                called out for that storm
                threatened but not coming
I came & came again
        imagining every hand of morning
        on me, opened my legs
        to the stupid sunrise
                giggling
                the both of us

I go a roving
        a roving
through troves of fathers
return with innumerable fathers
                small & clutching
my limbs, swinging
                what became of them?
they've told themselves off
& distant
& I only see them when I
                crack my knuckles

job well done, I'm telling myself
        value that rumor
        rumor is value
I see only what's been shown
a house painted so many times its
paint buckles
                in its inches
                        belts off circulation
numb, the painted house unwavering
its chimes are not alarms
a house wakes every hour on the hour

our names
        no longer important

                        I've lost track of
what I think you are

& now I've spent no time
                        it all comes back

Eavesdropped,
Paraphrased
(a thing between two pianos)

because of their factory jobs, pianos
rehearse only at night and on weekdays,
performances presented

only on Friday and Saturday nights
audience made up of
baking tins, and sewing machines

within architecturally
noteworthy buildings in a wide range of styles
coming from distinct time periods

later, they came to play in newer buildings
buildings which become an effort to memorialize
and rebuild, following the destruction of the originals

come to think of it, I've heard them
mentioned in the kitchen
come to think of it, there, a memory

one piano sighs to another
one never gets the kind of attention
they want these days

the other piano responds
the problem with getting what you
want is then wanting to want

Remembering For

shopping cart, worn clothing
empty lot but for the graffiti

flat against the wall
thinning contrast

f/ where
Where was I?

little odd scrapings of
pleasant

hello in the grocery store
whisperings of unquiet

I am twicely there
digital memory

this memory
everywhichthing unruly

I was born
in a town full of little odd

adjacencies to church
& I am no longer there but

break out the kitchen sink, honey
I'm not coming home

All Untouched

      my merry-go-round
    forever is today
more constant, more constant
      more sweet

less dry
where's the wine
       taken out
of my diet
    can I get on you?
   can I get on you
     & squeeze my legs round your
ribs & cackle while you whimper?
I only make bad jokes
    when I am now
      & tired
    & now

interderminable
la la
     I got this job sideways
   the ride from here to there
was drunk
   it gave me a shower
     took years to dry
     give up songs of you & me
& now I am quiet
    this space is new
between here & later
& then
  & then
    &then

Untitled

belittle only
        that which never changes
the title of this book
            has always been what it is
& so I will be little before it
      & make it
      match me
      slowly

The Burning House Has Few Rules

no burning in the burning house

do not mistake the burning house for metaphor, this results in the breaking of the first rule

do not breath fanatically, this fans flames, and quickens the end of the state of burning

do not fall in love inside the burning house, you will not get a sense of which burning is pertininent to which sensation

if you must smoke, do so with the windows closed, so as not to confuse the neighbors with multiple smokes rising

do not remove anything from the burning house, the burning house belongs to itself, and you and your things belong to the house and burning is no longer yours to concern yourself with

no burning without the burning house

Different Ways of Saying the Same Thing

    I am Crista
        I am Crista trying to be Crista
            I am Crista unlearning Crista trying to be Crista

        I am fumbling
        inside the noun that is my name
        I've taken comfort and terror
        from moments I am aware

        no one knows where I am

Falsity

fake under mattress
               marred
no springs
their absence gears
               turnings not our fault
               only our concern
& yes
be careful
               feathers are fake too
               beneath the pillow's cloth
      a scream jarred up

Repetition

grotesque is no longer
        grotesque
                shock constant & dim
if these objects continue to repeat
       I will no longer call them to me
          clusters of women are
                quietly laughing among themselves
                  carrying more things than one ought to be able
                        to carry–how uninteresting we can be
            is exciting
I look more & more
       at lovers' faces &
                              see semicolons with nothing
after, after this there is nothing
after this–each second is a ledge
       I look at my toes at the edge
       of the high dive & everything
is nothing is everything
is nothing but another kind
       of blue & hesitance
but there is something that always
       makes my decision for me
            I jump not knowing how
another second, another
      second, now now
            & I am never where I think I am

Prayer

grant me the where-
                                    with-all
to have all of it shimmering

glorious towns of
                  people procreating

                splendid
                night, a nerve with no end

this hand is not
                              always a hand
sometimes a question
        an unsituated grin

How Long a Road You Have in Those Feet?

        love has been told to me pretty but
found it gruesome
        if I tell you I love you anyway
                is it lost?
I go wayward to bend it out
I've not got the answer
said *same*
        when *different* you would've stayed
& stayed, I would have hungered you to bed
hungered your chest
        to hunger my back
                particular particularity
        a peculiar fashion
I've been so fragile
        left the window wide open
                for February to see
                if I could stand it
        to see a haunting of wine
        unsmell itself from my white blouse
but unkind examiner, February fell
me back
        into me
                so I am not so scary
        I lost my claws & teeth
                    softness found my hands and
                bounced me into here

Impossibility Grows into Night

        how willing stovetop
            how willing the fan
            how willing this form
    form down

lambent, fulgor nodule
            another shirtless man inhales
        branches
    while those
branches branch

quiddity, crux
bag of bones
    some sum of soma
        an intimidating subject of
            intimidating size

fervorless
overheard a voice from the twigs
        growing gloom I was unaware
            I stood naked this decade

found the exact urgency
        sleeping with the wisdom of a friend
    & nothing more
        forever wasted day, but no longer
    wasted through

Jacob's Ladder

        with my eyes
        closed used to be
                evidence I could commune
                      with a god somehow
                that beyond my desire for control
                there was an intuition blooming
        like how singular underwater I am held
        all at once
                but when I am alone, have
I vanished myself?

Pink

pink walls, pale in parts
        peeling & punctuated in oils, hand
                smudges, silverware stained with
residue–droplets from
                underperforming machine
glasses foggy with having been polished
            with filthy rags
       when water is poured in they smell
       again of the imperfect water they've soaked in
smells like the spit of strangers
I know the saliva of you
accustomed to it more quickly than others
                we resemble each other none the better for it

Sauna

I cannot be anyone
        only someone
but to be one at all
            is a trial
& I forgot
            my line
I don't have the
space to know who watches
I cave my caveable parts
        into majesty
                set the flowers down
where they can rot without
me–still I can't tell you
                why I had them
        colors of the afternoon
            insurmountable
yet never without motion
        in unstaring eye of a bleached
        midday summer sun
sons, I would if
        I had them
                go without them
to a sauna
        sweat them out of me
                go naked before
                broad windows, make
angels in steam
        lower myself down stairs
                into cold cold
                cylinder of water
never think again
        of what I could do for them
                only what I could
                      do for the impressions
                            of them that remained
                after I forget

The Kitchen Floor Was Fitting Once

for fucking, but now seems the stage
for waiting, this tea to cool, too cool now

goodbye, goodbye
I go, but only as you like
timid, there went solace

lost it to the wonder, meant only
to open up our fences to face
the east, as the east

can tell us something of
no, don't look, don't look
this way for now

Quiet

silence is not repeated but prolonged
a puddle connected below the pavement through the
dream I had & dove into and I am gliding still

songs are jumping into each other, mockery
of mockery of their own time
& synchronizing other times

I ring through the quiet
I continue on through
I am wriggling on these lines

Uncover My Covering

        of these pleasantries
        & I scare myself silly
no place to go from here

moving from alone to alone to
        not alone
        not alone to alone to alone
waking to sleeping

sleeping to waking
        all parts
        resisting, I resist
the turn we took to assholes

in the corner, but
        you can have these chairs
        emptied
flourescence

light tubes crossing
        dim reflection
        she walks forward interrupting
another crossing

while he also crosses himself
        over and over
        punctuation overused
it means nothing

breath, even this
        in need of moderation
        as they could lose themselves
to air in air aloft

Another Round

wheels go backward
        if you watch them   from an unflattering perspective
           they go as they were meant to, which was

                      going, which was
                      going to go when the going was good
            which was always when prompted

I never knew the way to the station
            I never knew the way to *the* station was only
a station not *the* station

I've made statements about *a* station that was not *the* station, still
        I would love to find it anyhow
                without all the wondering wandering between

Where Is My Imagery

> *where is my imagery*
> I got to sleep
middle finger still charcoaled
I've lost something in the
repetition
but have forgotten who to ask

which little god got inside me?
is it too dark in there to prevent
my collisions?

Goodbyes

within an unseemly encounter
its participants seem to one another
a great many things

they hope one day to move past
the seeming, but no
they've all been caught

without seam rippers, so
they will, they guess, remain unable
to unseem their meeting's stitches

www.ingramcontent.com/pod-product-compliance
Lightning Source LLC
Chambersburg PA
CBHW051807100526
44592CB00016B/2607